Recovery
A Lifelong
Journey

Juanita & Dale Ryan

6 Studies for
Groups or Individuals

With Notes for Leaders

✔ *L I F E R E C O V E R Y G U I D E S*

INTERVARSITY PRESS
DOWNERS GROVE, ILLINOIS 60515

InterVarsity Press® is the book-publishing division of InterVarsity Christian Fellowship®, a student movement active on campus at hundreds of universities, colleges and schools of nursing in the United States of America, and a member movement of the International Fellowship of Evangelical Students. For information about local and regional activities, write Public Relations Dept., InterVarsity Christian Fellowship, 6400 Schroeder Rd., P.O. Box 7895, Madison, WI 53707-7895.

All Scripture quotations, unless otherwise indicated, are taken from the HOLY BIBLE, NEW INTERNATIONAL VERSION®. NIV®. Copyright ©1973, 1978, 1984 by International Bible Society. Used by permission of Zondervan Publishing House. All rights reserved.

The Twelve Steps are reprinted with permission of Alcoholics Anonymous World Services, Inc. Permission to reprint and adapt the Twelve Steps does not mean that A.A. has reviewed or approved the contents of this publication, nor that A.A. agrees with the views expressed herein. A.A. is a program of recovery from alcoholism. Use of the Twelve Steps in connection with programs which are patterned after A.A. but which address other problems does not imply otherwise.

Cover illustration: Tim Nyberg

ISBN 0-8308-1166-4

Printed in the United States of America ∞

14	13	12	11	10	9	8	7	6	5	4	3	2	1
04	03	02	01	00	99	98	97	96	95	94	93		

An Invitation to Recovery

Life Recovery Guides are rooted in four basic convictions.

First, we are in need of recovery. The word *recovery* implies that something has gone wrong. Things are not as they should be. We have sinned. We have been sinned against. We are entangled, stuck, bogged down, bound and broken. We need to be healed.

Second, recovery is a commitment to change. Because of this, recovery is a demanding process and often a lengthy one. There are no quick fixes in recovery. It means facing the truth about ourselves, even when that truth is painful. It means giving up our old destructive patterns and learning new life-giving patterns. Recovery means taking responsibility for our lives. It is not easy. It is sometimes painful. And it will take time.

Third, recovery is possible. No matter how hopeless it may seem, no matter how deeply we have been wounded by life or how often we have failed, recovery is possible. Our primary basis for hope in the process of recovery is that God is able to do things which we cannot do ourselves. Recovery is possible because God has committed himself to us.

Finally, these studies are rooted in the conviction that the Bible can be a significant resource for recovery. Many people who have lived through difficult life experiences have had bits of the Bible thrown at their pain as a quick fix or a simplistic solution. As a result, many people expect the Bible to be a barrier to recovery rather than a resource. These studies are based on the belief that the

Bible is not a book of quick fixes and simplistic solutions. It is, on the contrary, a practical and helpful resource for recovery.

We were deeply moved personally by these biblical texts as we worked on this series. We are convinced that the God of the Bible can bring serenity to people whose lives have become unmanageable. If you are looking for resources to help you in your recovery, we invite you to study the Bible with an open mind and heart.

Getting the Most from Life Recovery Guides

Life Recovery Guides are designed to assist you to find out for yourself what the Bible has to say about different aspects of recovery. The texts you will study will be thought-provoking, challenging, inspiring and very personal. It will become obvious that these studies are not designed merely to convince you of the truthfulness of some idea. Rather, they are designed to allow biblical truths to renew your heart and mind.

We want to encourage realistic expectations of these discussion guides. First, they are not intended to be everything-the-Bible-says about any subject. They are not intended to be a systematic presentation of biblical theology.

Second, we want to emphasize that these guides are not intended to provide a recovery program or to be a substitute for professional counseling. If you are in a counseling relationship or are involved in a support group, we pray that these studies will enrich that resource. If you are not in a counseling relationship and your recovery involves long-term issues, we encourage you to consider seeking the assistance of a mental health professional.

What these guides are designed to do is to help you study a series of biblical texts which relate to the process of recovery. Our hope is that they will allow you to discover the Good News for people who are struggling to recover.

There are six studies in each Life Recovery Guide. This should provide you with maximum flexibility in how you use these guides.

Combining the guides in various ways will allow you to adapt them to your time schedule and to focus on the concerns most important to you or your group.

All of the studies in this series use a workbook format. Space is provided for writing answers to each question. This is ideal for personal study and allows group members to prepare in advance for the discussion. The guides also contain leader's notes with suggestions on how to lead a group discussion. The notes provide additional background information on certain questions, give helpful tips on group dynamics and suggest ways to deal with problems that may arise during the discussion. These features enable someone with little or no experience to lead an effective discussion.

Suggestions for Individual Study

1. As you begin each study, pray that God would bring healing and recovery to you through his Word.

2. After spending time in personal reflection, read and reread the passage to be studied.

3. Write your answers in the spaces provided or in a personal journal. Writing can bring clarity and deeper understanding of yourself and of the Bible. For the same reason, we suggest that you write out your prayers at the end of each study.

4. Use the leader's notes at the back of the guide to gain additional insight and information.

5. Share what you are learning with someone you trust. Recovery is empowered by experiences of community.

Suggestions for Group Study

Even if you have already done these studies individually, we strongly encourage you to find some way to do them with a group of other people as well. Although each person's recovery is different, everyone's recovery is empowered by the mutual support and encouragement that can only be found in a one-on-one or a group setting.

Several reminders may be helpful for participants in a group study:

1. Realize that trust grows over time. If opening up in a group setting is risky, realize that you do not have to share more than what feels safe to you. However, taking risks is a necessary part of recovery. So, do participate in the discussion as much as you are able.

2. Be sensitive to the other members of the group. Listen attentively when they talk. You will learn from their insights. If you can, link what you say to the comments of others so the group stays on the topic. Also, be affirming whenever you can. This will encourage some of the more hesitant members of the group to participate.

3. Be careful not to dominate the discussion. We are sometimes so eager to share what we have learned that we do not leave opportunity for others to respond. By all means participate! But allow others to do so as well.

4. Expect God to teach you through the passage being discussed and through the other members of the group. Pray that you will have a profitable time together.

5. We recommend that groups follow a few basic guidelines, and that these guidelines be read at the beginning of each discussion session. The guidelines, which you may wish to adapt to your situation, are:

  a. Anything said in the group is considered confidential and will not be discussed outside the group unless specific permission is given to do so.

  b. We will provide time for each person present to talk if he or she feels comfortable doing so.

  c. We will talk about ourselves and our own situations, avoiding conversation about other people.

  d. We will listen attentively to each other.

  e. We will be very cautious about giving advice.

  f. We will pray for each other.

If you are the discussion leader, you will find additional suggestions and helpful ideas for each study in the leader's notes. These are found at the back of the guide.

Introducing Recovery: A Lifelong Journey

"When will I ever be done with the hard work of recovery?" Jim asked. Discouragement and frustration were beginning to undermine his hopes for finding serenity.

"You need to remember that you have been practicing at being the way you are for many years," Bill responded. "It takes most of us quite a while to unlearn our addictive instincts. And then it takes a while longer to learn a healthier way of living. It will probably be easier if you come to see recovery not as something to get-done-with but as a whole new way of living."

Recovery is a lifelong journey. It is a task worthy of a lifetime to learn to live an honest and humble life, one day at a time, practicing the principles that lead to serenity. The Twelve Steps are a powerful set of biblical disciplines that can help us grow out of the addictive process into the freedom of God's grace. In the process we move away from toxic self-reliance and learn instead to turn our lives and wills over to God. We move away from dishonesty and learn instead to practice self-awareness and honest confession. We move away from pretense and learn instead to ask God to remove our shortcomings. We come to the end of blaming and instead accept responsibility for our wrongdoings. None of these changes are short-term. None are easy. They are changes for the long haul—changes we want to maintain for the rest of our lives because they bring us health and peace.

The Twelve Steps (see pp. 50-51 for a complete list of them) are a collection of traditional Christian spiritual disciplines that have helped many people grow in their relationship with God. They are a pathway to living at peace with God, at peace with ourselves and at peace with others. In *Recovery from Addictions* we examined some of the biblical foundations for the first three steps of the Twelve Steps. This foundational material teaches us how to make peace with God by admitting our need for God and by making a decision to turn our lives and wills over to God's care. In *Recovery from Guilt* we examined some of the biblical foundations for steps four through nine. The disciplines of these steps teach us how to make peace with ourselves and with others by admitting our wrongdoings, by asking God to change us and by making amends to people who we have harmed.

This Life Recovery Guide examines the biblical foundations for the last three of the Twelve Steps. Here we will learn the art of maintaining and deepening the recovery process that is starting to reshape our lives. These steps teach us to practice ongoing self-awareness, to continue to confess our wrongdoings, to seek a deeper relationship with God, to ask God for guidance, to share what we have received with others and to practice these principles in all parts of our life.

It has been said that health is more than the absence of illness. In the same way, recovery is more than the absence of addictive or compulsive behaviors. Recovery is a new way of life. It is a lifelong journey toward spiritual, emotional, physical and social wholeness. The prophet Micah once asked how we ought to live and came to the conclusion that we should seek "to act justly and to love mercy and to walk humbly with your God" (Micah 6:8). This wisdom for daily living is reflected in the last three of the Twelve Steps. Our journey through life can be characterized by acts of justice, the love of mercy and walking humbly with God.

It is our prayer that you will find deep joy and enduring peace as you continue on the lifelong journey of recovery.

May your roots sink deeply in the soil of God's love.

Juanita and Dale Ryan

1
Practicing Self-Awareness

"I guess the day was mixed, as usual," Ron said in answer to his friend's question. "I snapped at the kids when I got home from work, when the person I was really angry at was my boss. I felt bad about it, and I apologized to them. On the positive side, I did work today with a particularly difficult account, but I didn't lose my temper, and I was able to be more patient than I have been in the past. And, listening to myself talk just now encourages me to think that I am gradually becoming better at taking a daily inventory."

Taking a "searching moral inventory" is a critical part of the recovery process. Recovery does not come from working on other people's character defects or focusing on the things other people need to change. It is becoming aware of our own character defects and working on our own inventory that makes recovery possible. This does not, however, come easily for most of us. We must intentionally decide to give up living in the darkness of denial and ask God to illuminate our lives with truth. Step ten of the Twelve Steps is an invitation to practice this kind of honest self-awareness on a daily basis. It is honest self-examination and the resulting self-awareness which provides the necessary foundation for all change and growth.

It is important to remember that self-awareness has nothing to do with being selfish or with self-worship. It is quite the opposite. It is a humbling, often painful, but also exciting experience to face the truth about ourselves. The process of self-awareness is a process of paying attention to ourselves. It requires that we take time every day to reflect on our feelings, our thoughts, our behaviors, our desires. What are they? What are the needs for healing and change to which they point?

The spiritual disciplines which allow us to grow in self-awareness are varied. For most of us, however, it is helpful to make room in our lives for times of meditation, prayer and reflection. Many people find that keeping a journal is a helpful part of this process. When we rise in the morning, as we move through the day and as we lie in bed at night, we can ask God to show us what we need to know about ourselves in order to grow in our experience of God's healing, peace and joy.

☐ Personal Reflection _____

1. Do you find it easy or difficult to take time to pay attention to yourself? Explain.

2. What thoughts and feelings do you have about taking a personal inventory (step ten) on a regular basis?

3. What potential benefits do you think might come out of continuing to take a personal inventory?

☐ **Bible Study**————————————————————

Search me, O God, and know my heart;
   test me and know my anxious thoughts.
See if there is any offensive way in me,
   and lead me in the way everlasting. (Psalm 139:23-24)

1. What insights did you gain from your time of personal reflection?

2. The self-awareness which the psalmist desired is experienced in the context of a relationship with God. How has your relationship with God contributed to the growth of your self-awareness?

3. In this text the psalmist asks God to thoroughly examine his life.

What does this request suggest about the psalmist's relationship with God?

4. The psalmist asks God to "know my heart." Restate in your own words what you think he wants God to do.

5. The psalmist asks God to "know my anxious thoughts." Restate this request in your own words.

What anxious thoughts are you aware of at this time in your life?

6. The psalmist asks God if there is any "offensive way" in him. Restate this request in your own words.

What offensive ways is God showing you in your life?

7. The writer asks God to "lead me in the way everlasting." He is asking to be led in the way of life rather than in the way of death. How can denial and blame lead to death?

How can self-awareness lead to life?

8. Spend some time taking a personal inventory of your life from this day, and from this week.

☐ **Prayer** ⎯⎯⎯⎯⎯⎯⎯⎯⎯⎯⎯⎯⎯⎯⎯⎯⎯⎯⎯⎯⎯⎯⎯⎯⎯

What gift of self-awareness would you like to ask God to give you today?

2
Continuing
Confession

"What I said in front of the boss today was thoughtless and insensi-
tive," Dave said. "I put you down. I guess I did it to make myself
look good. I am sorry. With God's help, I will try to stop treating
you like this."

Joan was stunned. She had been hurt by Dave's comment, but she
had come to expect this kind of behavior from him. What she did
not expect was for him to be aware of what he was doing, admit it,
express regret and commit himself to change.

Our defensive instincts often keep us from seeing how our behaviors impact other people. We do something hurtful and then we try
to minimize it, adding a second injury to the first, and further dam-
aging our relationships.

The spiritual discipline of confession is at the heart of God's plan
for growing us into the kind of people who are capable of intimate
relationships. Step ten of the Twelve Steps teaches us to continue
this spiritual discipline on a daily basis. Instead of minimizing
our wrongdoings, or shaming ourselves for them, we are invited
to promptly admit them. We can clear the air. We can say the

truth to ourselves and to others.

Step ten of the Twelve Steps is an invitation to live vulnerable, open, honest lives. When we are wrong, we can promptly admit it.

☐ Personal Reflection _____

1. When you become aware of a way in which you have harmed another person, do you find it easy to promptly admit it? Why? Why not? Explain.

2. What benefits do you see to promptly admitting your wrongs?

3. What barriers might keep you from practicing the spiritual discipline of confession?

☐ Bible Study _____

Return, O Israel, to the LORD your God.
    Your sins have been your downfall!

Take words with you
   and return to the LORD.
Say to him:
   "Forgive all our sins
and receive us graciously,
   that we may offer the fruit of our lips."

"I will heal their waywardness
   and love them freely,
   for my anger has turned away from them." (Hosea 14:1-2, 4)

---

1. What insights did you gain from your time of personal reflection?

2. What images come to your mind when you read the phrase "Return to the Lord your God"?

3. The Lord says in this text, "Your sins have been your downfall." In what ways have your sins been your downfall?

4. The text tells us to "take words with us" when we return to the Lord. It then gives us words to say. What thoughts and feelings do you have in response to these words?

5. Restate in your own words what this text says God's response will be to us when we return to him.

6. What thoughts and feelings do you have about this response from God?

7. Spend some time picturing yourself returning to God, seeking forgiveness. Picture God healing the pain that continues to drive you to destructive behaviors. Picture God loving you freely. What responses do you have to this meditation?

8. What wrongs do you need to admit at this time?

☐ **Prayer** _____

What would you like to say to the God who loves you freely?

3
Seeking God

The heart of the healing journey is a growing relationship with God.
Fundamentally our problem is not alcohol, or sex, or food, or work,
or drugs—our fundamental problem is spiritual impoverishment.
The heart of recovery is not, therefore, saying no to an addictive
substance or an addictive process. The heart of recovery is saying yes
to God.

The recovery journey begins when we admit our need for God,
acknowledge God's power, and make a decision to turn our lives and
wills over to God's care. But the beginning of the journey is just
that—the beginning. Growing in our relationship with God is a
journey of a lifetime. This is a very basic biblical truth—we can
grow; we can mature in our relationship with God. The way we
understand God now will give way to a fuller understanding as we
grow in faith. God seeks through a lifelong spiritual journey to grow
us into the kind of people who are capable of deeply intimate relationships. Those of us who have learned how to have relationships
with little "conscious contact" will have a lot to learn in the process.

Step eleven of the Twelve Steps teaches us that powerful resources for this lifelong spiritual journey are found in the conscious contact with God made possible by prayer and meditation. Christian prayer and Christian meditation are not easy disciplines. Many of us have used prayer as a magical device for controlling God or for acquiring God's favor. Similarly, many use meditation as a magical tool for control. But there is nothing magical about the spiritual disciplines of prayer and meditation. Both are ways to focus our attention on God. We can talk (pray) openly, honestly, vulnerably to God, and we can listen (meditate) with humility. It is this dynamic of speaking/listening, prayer/meditation that makes it possible for us to increase our contact with God. We can experience loving and being loved by our Creator.

☐ Personal Reflection ————————————————————————————

1. Describe your current practices of prayer and meditation.

2. What difficulties do you experience with prayer and meditation?

3. What changes, if any, would you like to make in these practices?

4. What thoughts and feelings do you have when you think of seeking to improve your contact with God?

☐ **Bible Study**_____

I am laid low in the dust;
 preserve my life according to your word.
I recounted my ways and you answered me;
 teach me your decrees.
Let me understand the teaching of your precepts;
 then I will meditate on your wonders.
My soul is weary with sorrow;
 strengthen me according to your word.
Keep me from deceitful ways;
 be gracious to me through your law.
I have chosen the way of truth;
 I have set my heart on your laws.
I hold fast to your statutes, O LORD;
 do not let me be put to shame.
I run in the path of your commands,
 for you have set my heart free.

Teach me, O LORD, to follow your decrees;
 then I will keep them to the end.
Give me understanding, and I will keep your law
 and obey it with all my heart.
Direct me in the path of your commands,
 for there I find delight.
Turn my heart toward your statutes

and not toward selfish gain.
Turn my eyes away from worthless things;
  preserve my life according to your word. (Psalm 119:25-37)

---

1. What insights did you gain from your time of personal reflection?

2. Restate in your own words the requests the psalmist makes of God.

3. What major needs/desires is the psalmist expressing in these requests?

4. How do these needs/desires compare with your own needs/desires at this time?

5. Which of these requests would you most like to make of God at this time? Explain.

6. The psalmist describes himself as "laid low in the dust" and as "weary with sorrow." Describe a time when you experienced these feelings.

7. How does the psalmist describe what he has done and what he desires to do in his pursuit of God?

8. What benefits does the psalmist suggest might come from prayer and meditation?

9. In your experience, how can prayer and meditation improve our contact with God?

☐ **Prayer** ————————————————————————————

Write a prayer asking God to help you practice the disciplines of prayer and meditation.

4
Asking
for Guidance

"The way I was taught to pray," explained Sue, *"was to list for God* the things I wanted done. I would give God a long list of 'requests' that were really thinly disguised expectations or demands. It amazes me now, but I really felt I knew what everyone needed and that my job was to bring these needs to God's attention. I would decide what needed to be done and God would do it. Sound backwards? I think so. When I came to step eleven of the Twelve Steps, I was surprised to discover a humbler way to pray. I learned to say 'show me your will today and give me the power to carry it out.' I stopped telling God what to do and started to ask for guidance and help. Now I pray with an awareness that I am talking to my Creator, who knows me better than I know me, who loves me more than I love me, and who is personally involved in my life."

The kind of prayer suggested in step eleven of the Twelve Steps keeps us oriented to reality. It helps us to stay clear about who is God and who is not God. Asking to be shown God's will and asking for God to give us the power to carry it out reminds us that we are the dependent ones in need of wisdom and strength. It reminds us that serenity in life comes from daily acknowledging our need to let God be in charge of our lives.

Step eleven can be a very difficult part of the recovery journey. The spiritual roots of our desire to control will be exposed and confronted. The battle between our will and God's may become acute. But seeing clearly that we are not God can open us to new horizons of spiritual experience. And experiencing God's power to carry out God's purposes can be a powerfully transforming experience.

☐ Personal Reflection ———————————————————————

1. What might motivate you to desire to know God's will?

2. What fears might keep you from seeking to know and to do God's will?

☐ Bible Study ———————————————————————————

Answer me quickly, O LORD;
   my spirit faints with longing.
Do not hide your face from me
   or I will be like those who go down to the pit.
Let the morning bring me word of your unfailing love,
   for I have put my trust in you.
Show me the way I should go,

for to you I lift up my soul.
Rescue me from my enemies, O LORD,
    for I hide myself in you.
Teach me to do your will,
    for you are my God;
may your good Spirit
    lead me on level ground.

For your name's sake, O LORD, preserve my life;
    in your righteousness, bring me out of trouble. (Psalm 143:7-11)

---

1. What insights did you gain from your time of personal reflection?

2. What specifically does the psalmist say he longs for in the beginning of this text?

What does the psalmist fear might happen?

3. The psalmist asks for knowledge of God's will and the power to carry it out. What specifically does he ask for?

4. Which of these requests for direction and help do you especially identify with at this time? Explain.

5. The psalmist reminds God: "I have put my trust in you; to you I lift up my soul; I hide myself in you." What do you think the psalmist is trying to communicate to God?

6. In what area of life do you feel a need for knowledge of God's will?

7. What knowledge of God's will have you received, but are hesitant, and needing power, to carry out?

☐ **Prayer** _____

What guidance would you like to ask God for today?

5
Carrying the Message to Others

"I'm not sure what to tell you," Barb hesitated. *It was her first attempt* to share her story of recovery from compulsive eating with her friend Jan. "My relationship with food was completely out of control. Food was the most important thing in my life. I hated it and the incredible shame I felt before and after a binge. I finally went to a Twelve-Step meeting and when I heard them talk about being powerless over food, I knew what they were talking about. I knew I was unable to change my addiction by my own power. It may not sound like much, but it was the beginning for me of learning to tell the truth. I used to feel numb or asleep spiritually and now I am beginning to feel like I'm waking up. And that feels very good."

Step twelve of the Twelve Steps calls us to commit ourselves to building relationships with others. We are to "carry the message" of our spiritual awakening to others. It is important to emphasize that when we carry the message we are practicing the same disciplines of "truth-telling" which we learned in earlier steps of the Twelve-Step process. Step twelve does not tell us that we are responsible for someone else's recovery. It does not encourage us to present a carefully crafted "before" and "after" picture, in which we pretend that we no longer have problems. Step twelve is not about having a "good" testimony. It is about having an honest one.

Carrying the message to others involves a humble, honest sharing of our need for God and of our experience of God's power and commitment to us. Step twelve can be a very difficult part of the recovery journey. It requires us to learn to focus on the needs and concerns of others without losing the new self-awareness on which our own recovery is based. But step twelve can also be one of the most rewarding parts of the recovery journey. As we reach out to others with the message of hope, we will find ourselves renewed again and again in gratitude for God's grace-full love for us.

☐ Personal Reflection ————————————————————

1. Who "carried the message" of God's love and healing power to you?

2. How did they convey this message to you?

☐ Bible Study————————————————————————

Therefore, if anyone is in Christ, he is a new creation; the old has gone, the new has come! All this is from God, who reconciled us to himself through Christ and gave us the ministry of reconciliation: that God was reconciling the world to himself in Christ, not counting men's sins against them. And he has committed to us the message of reconciliation. We are therefore Christ's ambassadors, as though God were making his appeal through us. We implore you on Christ's behalf: Be reconciled to God. (2 Corinthians 5:17-20)

---

1. What insights did you gain from your time of personal reflection?

2. The text says that in Christ we are new creations, the "old has gone and the new has come." What does it mean to be a new creation in Christ?

How have you experienced newness in Christ?

3. Briefly write the story of your personal experience of "God reconciling you to himself through Christ." Include whatever experiences you have had with recovery from addictions, compulsions or codependency.

4. This text says that we have a message to carry to others. The language the text uses to describe the message is that "God is reconciling the world to himself in Christ, not counting men's sins against them." To reconcile is to bring enemies together as friends. We have treated God as an enemy. We have run from God. God has made it possible for us to be together again. Use this image of reconciliation to picture God's love for you. Imagine God throwing his arms around you in an enthusiastic, joyful hug. Imagine yourself allowing God to do so. What thoughts and feelings do you have in response to this image?

5. The text calls us to the "ministry of reconciliation." How have you experienced being a minister of reconciliation?

What might you do as a minister of reconciliation?

6. In your own words, briefly write the message you believe God would like you to carry to others.

7. How would you like to communicate this message?

8. What barriers (internal or external) stand in your way?

9. What positive experiences might come for you as a result of carrying the message to others?

☐ **Prayer** _____

What would you like to say to the God who has restored relationship with you through Christ?

6
Practicing the Principles

"I started to work the Twelve Steps because my life was out of control," Steve explained. "I was desperate. At the time, I thought that the steps were a kind of psychological technique designed simply to help me stop my addictive behavior. But I have learned that the simple wisdom of the steps applies to all of my affairs. The honesty, the humility, the dependence on God that made my recovery possible are important in all of my relationships and in everything that I do."

The principles expressed in the Twelve Steps are the life-giving principles of the gospel. We need God. Every day we make the decision to turn our lives over to God's care. Every day we practice self-awareness, honesty, confession and amend-making. Every day we seek contact with God and ask for knowledge of God's will for us, through prayer and meditation. Every day we open ourselves to the possibility of sharing the story of God's love with others.

Every day, in all our affairs, we can practice the wisdom of these principles.

□ **Personal Reflection** ———————————————

1. Briefly summarize the principles of the Twelve Steps as you see them (see pages 50-51 for a complete list of the Twelve Steps).

2. Which of these principles has been especially difficult for you? Explain.

3. Which of these principles has been especially life-changing for you? Explain.

□ **Bible Study**———————————————

You, my brothers, were called to be free. But do not use your freedom to indulge the sinful nature; rather, serve one another in love. The entire law is summed up in a single command: "Love your neighbor as yourself." If you keep on biting and devouring each other, watch out or you will be destroyed by each other. So I say, live by the Spirit, and you will not gratify the desires of the sinful nature. For the sinful nature desires what is contrary to the Spirit, and the Spirit what is contrary to the sinful nature. They are in conflict with each other, so that you do not do what you want. But if you are led by the Spirit, you are not under law. The acts of the sinful nature are obvious: sexual immorality, impurity and debauchery; idolatry and witchcraft; hatred, discord, jealousy, fits of rage, selfish ambition, dissensions, factions and envy; drunkenness, orgies, and the like. I warn you, as I did before, that those who live like this will not inherit the kingdom of God. But the fruit of the Spirit is love, joy, peace, patience, kindness, goodness, faithfulness, gentleness and self-control. Against such things there is no law. (Galatians 5:13-23)

---

1. What insights did you gain from your time of personal reflection?

2. The text begins with a remarkable statement: "You were called to be free." What new freedom have you experienced as a result of God's healing in your life?

3. According to this text, God's law can be summed up in a single command: "Love your neighbor as yourself." What practical meaning does this have for you?

What overlap do you see between the principles of the Twelve Steps and loving your neighbor as yourself?

4. The text contrasts "loving each other" with "devouring and destroying each other." How do addictions and compulsions lead to devouring and destroying?

5. Restate in your own words the description the text gives of the "acts of the sinful nature."

6. What relationship do you see between these acts and addictive or compulsive behaviors?

7. List the nine qualities the Spirit brings into our lives. Next to each character quality make a note of a time when you experienced this work of the Spirit in your life in the recent past.

8. Which of these qualities would you especially like the Spirit to grow in you at this time?

9. Picture yourself as a tree, deeply rooted in the soil of God's love, growing strong and healthy. Picture God's Spirit moving through your branches, producing beautiful fruit. What thoughts and feelings do you have about this image?

☐ **Prayer** _____

What help do you need from God in practicing the principles today?

Leader's Notes

You may be experiencing a variety of feelings as you anticipate leading a group using a Life Recovery Guide. You may feel inadequate for the task and afraid of what will happen. If this is the case, know you are in good company. Many of the kings, prophets and apostles in the Bible felt inadequate and afraid. Many other small group leaders share this experience of fear as well.

Your willingness to lead, however, is a gift to the other group members. It might help if you tell them about your feelings and ask them to pray for you. Keep in mind that the other group members share the responsibility for the group. And realize that it is God's work to bring insight, comfort, healing and recovery to group members. Your role is simply to provide guidance to the discussion. The suggestions listed below will help you to provide that guidance.

Using the Life Recovery Guides

This Life Recovery Guide is one in a series of guides. The series was designed to be a flexible tool that can be used in various combinations by individuals and groups—such as support groups, Bible studies and Sunday-school classes. All of the guides in this series are designed to be useful to anyone. Each guide has a specific focus, but all are written with a general audience in mind.

Many congregation-based recovery ministries use the Life Recovery Guides as part of the curriculum for "newcomers" groups. It can be a critical step in the recovery process to recognize that "recovery" is not a new set of ideas or the latest trend in popular psychology. Finding that the Bible is attentive to our struggles can often provide the courage needed to continue when the journey becomes painful.

We strongly recommend that careful attention be given to the group dynamics of the Bible study. Traditional Bible studies in the Christian community tend to be cognitively oriented, leadership tends to be well defined, commenting on statements by other participants is usually encouraged, giving advice is often valued, and sharing concerns expressed in the group with nonparticipants is often understood to be a kind of caring. Special attention will often be needed, therefore, to use the Life Recovery Guides in a way that teaches group participants the norms, values and group dynamics of the support group ministry to which the person is being introduced.

For example, if the Life Recovery Guides are used as an introductory experience that leads toward participation in a Twelve-Step group, then the group dynamics should probably resemble as much as possible those of a Twelve-Step group. Group facilitators should take time to carefully explain the purpose of the group and to introduce group participants to new group norms. It will probably take some time and practice, for example, to assimilate the concept of "cross talk." Groups using the Life Recovery Guides can help build a biblical foundation for what follows in the recovery process. But they can also help people to develop the skills needed to benefit from a support group experience.

Each guide contains six studies. If eight guides are used, they can provide a year-long curriculum series. Or if the guides are used in pairs, they can provide studies for a quarter (twelve weeks). The following are some ways that you might find it helpful to use the guides in combination with one another:

Topic	Number of Studies/Weeks	Guides to Use
Introduction to Recovery	12	Recovery from Distorted Images of God
		Recovery from Distorted Images of Self
Abuse	30	Recovery from Abuse
		Recovery from Shame
		Recovery from Distorted Images of Self
		Recovery from Fear
		Recovery from Spiritual Abuse
Addictions	30	Recovery from Addictions (Steps 1-3)
		Recovery from Guilt (Steps 4-9)
		Recovery: A Lifelong Journey (Steps 10-12)
		Recovery from Codependency
		Recovery from Workaholism
Family Dysfunctions	18	Recovery from Family Dysfunctions
		Recovery from Distorted Images of God
		Recovery from Distorted Images of Self
Divorce	30	Recovery from Depression
		Recovery from Loss
		Recovery from Shame
		Recovery from Broken Relationships
		Recovery from Bitterness
Grief and Loss	24	Recovery from Loss
		Recovery from Fear
		Recovery from Depression
		Recovery from Distorted Images of God

Preparing to Lead

1. Develop realistic expectations of yourself as a small group leader. Do not feel that you have to "have it all together." Rather, commit yourself to an ongoing discipline of honesty about your own needs. As you grow in honesty about your own needs, you will grow as well in your capacity for compassion, gentleness and patience with yourself and with others. As a leader, you can encourage an atmosphere of honesty by being honest about yourself.

2. Pray. Pray for yourself and your own recovery. Pray for the group members. Invite the Holy Spirit to be present as you prepare and as you meet.

3. Read the study several times.

4. Take your time to thoughtfully work through each question, writing out your answers.

5. After completing your personal study, read through the leader's notes for the study you are leading. These notes are designed to help you in several ways. First, they tell you the purpose the authors had in mind while writing the study. Take time to think through how the questions work together to accomplish that purpose. Second, the notes provide you with additional background information or comments on some of the questions. This information can be useful if people have difficulty understanding or answering a question. Third, the leader's notes can alert you to potential problems you may encounter during the study.

6. If you wish to remind yourself during the group discussion of anything mentioned in the leader's notes, make a note to yourself below that question in your study guide.

Leading the Study

1. Begin on time. You may want to open in prayer, or have a group member do so.

2. Be sure everyone has a study guide. Decide as a group if you want people to do the study on their own ahead of time. If your time together is limited, it will be helpful for people to prepare in advance.

3. At the beginning of your first time together, explain that these studies are meant to be discussions, not lectures. Encourage the members of the group to participate. However, do not put pressure on those who may be hesitant to speak during the first few sessions. Clearly state that people do not need to share anything they do not feel safe sharing. Remind people that it will take time to trust each other.

4. Read aloud the group guidelines listed in the front of the guide. These commitments are important in creating a safe place for people to talk and trust and feel.

5. The covers of the Life Recovery Guides are designed to incorporate both symbols of the past and hope for the future. During your first meeting, allow the group to describe what they see in the cover and respond to it.

6. Read aloud the introductory paragraphs at the beginning of the discussion for the day. This will orient the group to the passage being studied.

7. The personal reflection questions are designed to help group members focus on some aspect of their experience. Hopefully, they will help group members to be more aware of the frame of reference and life experience which they bring to the study. The personal reflection section can be done prior to the group meeting or as the first part of the meeting. If the group does not prepare in advance, approximately ten minutes will be needed for individuals to consider these questions.

The personal reflection questions are not designed to be used directly for group discussion. Rather, the first question in the Bible study section is intended to give group members an opportunity to reveal what they feel safe sharing from their time of personal reflection.

8. Read the passage aloud. You may choose to do this yourself, or prior to the study you might ask someone else to read.

9. As you begin to ask the questions in the guide, keep several things in mind. First, the questions are designed to be used just as they are written. If you wish, you may simply read them aloud to the group. Or you may prefer to express them in your own words. However, unnecessary rewording of the questions is not recommended.

Second, the questions are intended to guide the group toward understanding and applying the main idea of the study. You will find the purpose of each study described in the leader's notes. You should try to understand how the study questions and the biblical text work together to lead the group in that direction.

There may be times when it is appropriate to deviate from the study guide. For example, a question may have already been answered. If so, move on to the next question. Or someone may raise an important question not covered in the guide. Take time to discuss it! The important thing is to use discretion. There may be many routes you can travel to reach the goal of the study. But the easiest route is usually the one we have suggested.

10. Don't be afraid of silence. People need time to think about the question before formulating their answers.

11. Draw out a variety of responses from the group. Ask, "Who else has some thoughts about this?" or "How did some of the rest of you respond?" until several people have given answers to the question.

12. Acknowledge all contributions. Try to be affirming whenever possible. Never reject an answer. If it seems clearly wrong to you, ask, "Which part of the text led you to that conclusion?" or "What do the rest of you think?"

13. Realize that not every answer will be addressed to you, even though this will probably happen at first. As group members become more at ease, they will begin to interact more effectively with each other. This is a sign of a healthy discussion.

14. Don't be afraid of controversy. It can be very stimulating. Differences can enrich our lives. If you don't resolve an issue completely, don't be frustrated. Move on and keep it in mind for later. A subsequent study may resolve the problem. Or, the issue may not be resolved—not all questions have answers!

15. Stick to the passage under consideration. It should be the source for answering the questions. Discourage the group from unnecessary cross-referencing. Likewise, stick to the subject and avoid going off on tangents.

16. Periodically summarize what the group has said about the topic. This helps to draw together the various ideas mentioned and gives

continuity to the study. But be careful not to use summary statements as an opportunity to give a sermon!

17. During the discussion, feel free to share your own responses. Your honesty about your own recovery can set a tone for the group to feel safe in sharing. Be careful not to dominate the time, but do allow time for your own needs as a group member.

18. Each study ends with a time for prayer. There are several ways to handle this time in a group. The person who leads each study could lead the group in a prayer or you could allow time for group participation. Remember that some members of your group may feel uncomfortable about participating in public prayer. It might be helpful to discuss this with the group during your first meeting and to reach some agreement about how to proceed.

19. Realize that trust in a group grows over time. During the first couple meetings, people will be assessing how safe they will feel in the group. Do not be discouraged if people share only superficially at first. The level of trust will grow slowly but steadily.

Listening to Emotional Pain

Life Recovery Guides are designed to take seriously the pain and struggle that is part of life. People will experience a variety of emotions during these studies. Your role as group leader is not to act as a professional counselor. Instead it is to be a friend who listens to emotional pain. Listening is a gift you can give to hurting people. For many, it is not an easy gift to give. The following suggestions can help you listen more effectively to people in emotional pain.

1. Remember that you are not responsible to take the pain away. People in helping relationships often feel that they are being asked to make the other person feel better. This is usually related to the helper's own patterns of not being comfortable with painful feelings.

2. Not only are you not responsible to take the pain away, one of the things people need most is an opportunity to face and to experience the pain in their lives. They have usually spent years denying their pain and running from it. Healing can come when we are able to face our pain in the presence of someone who cares about us. Rather than trying to take the pain away, commit yourself to listening attentively as it is expressed.

3. Realize that some group members may not feel comfortable with expressions of sadness or anger. You may want to acknowledge that such emotions are uncomfortable, but remind the group that part of recovery is to learn to feel and to allow others to feel.

4. Be very cautious about giving answers and advice. Advice and answers may make you feel better or feel competent, but they may also minimize people's problems and their painful feelings. Simple solutions rarely work, and they can easily communicate "You should be better now" or "You shouldn't really be talking about this."

5. Be sure to communicate direct affirmation any time people talk about their painful emotions. It takes courage to talk about our pain because it creates anxiety for us. It is a great gift to be trusted by those who are struggling.

The Twelve Steps of Alcoholics Anonymous

1. We admitted we were powerless over alcohol—that our lives had become unmanageable.

2. Came to believe that a Power greater than ourselves could restore us to sanity.

3. Made a decision to turn our will and our lives over to the care of God as we understood Him.

4. Made a searching and fearless moral inventory of ourselves.

5. Admitted to God, to ourselves, and to another human being the exact nature of our wrongs.

6. Were entirely ready to have God remove all these defects of character.

7. Humbly asked Him to remove our shortcomings.

8. Made a list of all persons we had harmed, and became willing to make amends to them all.

9. Made direct amends to such people wherever possible, except when to do so would injure them or others.

10. Continued to take personal inventory and when we were wrong promptly admitted it.

11. Sought through prayer and meditation to improve our conscious contact with God as we understood Him, praying only for knowledge of His will for us and the power to carry that out.

12. Having had a spiritual awakening as the result of these steps, we tried to carry this message to alcoholics, and to practice these principles in all our affairs.

See copyright page for Twelve Step credit line.

The following notes refer to the questions in the Bible study portion of each study:

Study 1. Practicing Self-Awareness. Psalm 139:23-24.

Purpose: To learn the value of practicing self-awareness.

Question 2. Self-awareness does not require us to become the focal point of the universe. Healthy self-awareness is made possible by healthy relationships. This is especially true of our relationship with God. Because of past pain, we may see God as a critical, judging, abusive, abandoning person. The process of coming to know God as an understanding, loving, nurturing parent parallels the process of becoming self-aware. As we find the courage to know ourselves, we grow in our awareness of God's love and care. And, as we experience God's love and care, we find the courage to become self-aware.

Question 3. The psalmist must have seen God as loving in some very specific ways. He saw God as intimately acquainted with him, as personally attentive to him, as personally involved in his life and as trustworthy.

Question 4. "Know my heart" could be paraphrased as "know my motives, know my secret thoughts, know my deepest longings and needs and feelings." People whose boundaries have been violated may find it difficult to relate to the psalmist's desire to be known in this way. But secrets are what undermine all intimate relationships. The psalmist is saying that he wants his relationship with God to be an intimate one.

Question 5. Usually our anxious thoughts concern the things in life over which we have no control. Anxious thoughts can immobilize us; they can become obsessive. They are reminders of our dependency on God. Our only real choice is to give our anxious thoughts to God and to make the decision, once again, to turn our lives over to God's care.

Question 6. Offensive ways are the things we do that are harmful to ourselves or to others. They are our shortcomings, our wrongdoings, our sins. Learning that God can be trusted with the worst information about us is not easy. Clearly the psalmist believes that God will not use this information against him. He expects God to be helpful.

Question 7. Denial and blame are defenses that keep us from seeing our addictions, our sin, our destructive ways. When we do not see these realities, we are doomed to continue in them. Self-awareness leads to life because (1) it allows us to see the areas in our life that need changing and healing, and (2) it keeps us in tune with our need to depend on God.

Question 8. If you are doing this study in a group, we encourage you to take the time for group members to share whatever parts of this exercise they want to. Alternatively, you can allow group time for the exercise, and then ask group participants what they found helpful or difficult about taking a daily inventory.

Study 2. Continuing Confession. Hosea 14:1-2, 4.

Purpose: To see the importance of continuing confession.

Question 2. The image of returning to the Lord is one of changing directions, of going back. We have wandered off, or gone off in anger, or in desperation. We have turned away from God. It is time now to turn back to him; to make a 180-degree turn; to admit our need of God; to confess the behaviors that caused us to turn away from God. Returning is going home again to the place where our hearts belong, to the place where we are always welcomed back.

Question 5. God says he will heal our waywardness. "Waywardness is a turning away from what is in our best interest to follow depraved, capricious inclinations. There are many ways in which waywardness can be expressed. Some of us are openly rebellious. We flaunt our wild behavior and laugh at God. Others of us are quietly wayward. We try to appear compliant and good but inside we are defiantly independent. No matter how we express our waywardness, it is a destructive force in our lives" (Ryan and Ryan, *Rooted in God's Love,* p. 171). God says he will love us freely. He will love us generously, completely, until our fears are calmed and our defenses are lowered. He will heal us with his generous love.

Question 8. If you are a group leader, depending on the level of trust and confidentiality which has formed in your group, you may want to ask group members to share whatever they choose with your group at this time. Alternatively, this exercise can be done in writing, followed by discussion of what was helpful or difficult about this exercise.

Study 3. Seeking God. Psalm 119:25-37.

Purpose: To experience a closer relationship with God.

Question 2. The psalmist asks God to (1) preserve his life, (2) teach him God's decrees, (3) let him understand the teaching, (4) strengthen him according to God's Word, (4) keep him from deceitful ways, (5) be gracious to him through the law, (6) not let him be put to shame, (7) direct his path to God's commands, (8) turn his heart to God's statutes, (9) turn his heart away from selfish gain, and (10) turn his eyes away from worthless things.

Question 7. The psalmist says: (1) I recounted my ways; (2) I will meditate on your wonders; (3) I have chosen the way of truth; (4) I have set my heart on your laws; (5) I hold fast to your statutes;

(6) I run in the path of your commands; (7) I will keep your law and obey it with all my heart; and (8) I find delight in your commands.

Question 8. The psalmist says "you have set my heart free." There is a quality of integrity, of connection to God, of freedom and of joy that comes from the practice of prayer and meditation in the pursuit of God.

Study 4. Asking for Guidance. Psalm 143:7-11.

Purpose: To learn a humble form of prayer.

Question 2. The psalmist longs for God (1) to show himself, (2) to "not hide his face from him," and (3) to send word of his unfailing love. The psalmist longs for God in a deeply personal way.

If God is distant, the psalmist fears that he will die, that he will "be like those who go down to the pit." The psalmist is acutely aware of his need for God's involvement in his life; he knows that he is dependent on God for his very life. He deeply fears being abandoned by God.

Question 3. The psalmist requests of God: "show me the way I should go," "rescue me from my enemies," "teach me to do your will," "lead me on a level ground," "preserve my life," and "bring me out of trouble."

Question 5. These are images of dependency and need. The psalmist seems to be saying, "I need you, God, I am relying on you, I am depending on you, please help me, please guide me, please come through for me."

Study 5. Carrying the Message to Others. 2 Corinthians 5:17-20.

Purpose: To see the importance of carrying the message to others.

Question 2. Being a new creation in Christ is a powerful image of being remade, of being reborn, of being rescued from death and given life. The text talks about this as an experience of the old being gone and the new coming. Christ brings about radical changes in our lives, replacing our addictions and compulsions with freedom and joy.

Question 4. The text says that God "has committed to us the message of reconciliation." And that we are "Christ's ambassadors, as though God were making his appeal through us." Reconciliation has to do with bringing enemies back together again. "Now the way to overcome enmity is to take away the cause of the quarrel. . . . The way to reconciliation lies through an effective grappling with the root cause of the enmity. Christ died to put away our sin. In this way He dealt with the enmity between man and God. He put it out of the way. He makes the way wide open for men to come back to God. It is this which is described by the term 'reconciliation' " (J. D. Douglas, ed., *The New Bible Dictionary* [Wheaton, Ill.: Tyndale, 1962], p. 1077). The text describes the message as the good news that "God is reconciling the world to himself in Christ, not counting men's sins against them."

Study 6. Practicing the Principles. Galatians 5:13-23.

Purpose: To apply the principles of the Twelve Steps to all areas of our life.

Question 3. Loving others has to do with valuing them, respecting them, being merciful toward them, wanting good things for them, being concerned for their welfare, caring about them. It is part of our growth and healing that we learn to value and respect ourselves so we can more fully value and respect others.

The principles of the Twelve Steps teach us (1) that we need help from God to live our lives and (2) that we need to stop blaming others and begin taking responsibility for our own behaviors. Both the Twelve Steps and the wisdom of "loving your neighbor" imply responsibility to act in loving ways toward others and when we do not, to acknowledge our shortcomings, to seek God's help to change and to make amends to the people we have harmed.

Question 4. Addictions and compulsions lead to devouring and destroying because our drug of choice becomes more important than the people in our lives. Instead of loving our neighbor as ourselves, we are loving neither our neighbor nor ourselves. We are pursuing behaviors that are destructive to ourselves and destructive to our relationships.

Question 5. The text lists the acts of the sinful nature as "sexual immorality, impurity and debauchery; idolatry and witchcraft; hatred, discord, jealousy, fits of rage, selfish ambition, dissensions, factions and envy; drunkenness, orgies, and the like."

Question 6. The acts of the sinful nature sound like (1) sexual addictions (sexual immorality, impurity, debauchery, orgies); (2) rage addictions (hatred, discord, jealousy, fits of rage, dissensions, factions, envy); (3) chemical addictions (drunkenness); and (4) work addictions (selfish ambition).

For more information about Christian resources for people in recovery and subscription information for STEPS, *the newsletter of the National Association for Christian Recovery, we invite you to write to:*

The National Association for Christian Recovery
P.O. Box 11095
Whittier, California 90603

LIFE RECOVERY GUIDES FROM INTER-VARSITY PRESS
By Dale and Juanita Ryan

Recovery from Abuse. Does the nightmare of abuse ever end? After emotional, verbal and/or physical abuse how can you develop secure relationships? Recovery is difficult but possible. This guide will help you turn to God as you put the broken pieces of your life back together again. Six studies, 64 pages, 1158-3.

Recovery from Addictions. Addictions have always been part of the human predicament. Chemicals, food, people, sex, work, spending, gambling, religious practices and more can enslave us. This guide will help you find the wholeness and restoration that God offers to those who are struggling with addictions. Six studies, 64 pages, 1155-9.

Recovery from Bitterness. Sometimes forgiveness gets blocked, stuck, restrained and entangled. We find our hearts turning toward bitterness and revenge. Our inability to forgive can make us feel like spiritual failures. This guide will help us find the strength to change bitterness into forgiveness. Six studies, 64 pages, 1154-0.

Recovery from Broken Relationships. Divorce. Family conflict. Death. We may learn to fear closeness because we don't want to experience another separation from someone we love. God wants to heal us of the pain of lost relationships. These studies help us discover how to risk love again and build healthy relationships that will endure. Six studies, 64 pages, 1165-6.

Recovery from Codependency. The fear, anger and helplessness people feel when someone they love is addicted can lead to desperate attempts to take care of, or control, the loved one. Both the addicted person's behavior and the frenzied codependent behavior progress in a destructive downward spiral of denial and blame. This guide will help you to let go of over-responsibility and entrust the people you love to God. Six studies, 64 pages, 1156-7.

Recovery from Depression. From time to time we all experience feelings of hopelessness in response to difficult events in life—broken relationships, death, unemployment and so on. Sometimes we are not able to work through those feelings alone. And we need to be pointed toward the source of hope. This guide will show you the way. Six studies, 64 pages, 1161-3.

Recovery from Distorted Images of God. In a world of sin and hate it is difficult for us to understand who the God of love is. These distortions interfere with our ability to express our feelings to God and to trust him. This guide helps us to identify the distortions we have and to come to a new understanding of who God is. Six studies, 64 pages, 1152-4.

Recovery from Distorted Images of Self. God created us as people who are to be loved, valued and capable. But sometimes we don't *feel* that we are really cared for. We mentally replay negative feedback again and again. These studies will show you how to escape those negatives and be restored to a true vision of yourself as a person of immense worth. Six studies, 64 pages, 1162-1.

Recovery from Family Dysfunctions. Dysfunctional patterns of relating learned early in life affect all of our relationships. We trust God and others less than we wish. This guide offers healing from the pain of the past and acceptance into God's family. Six studies, 64 pages, 1151-6.

Recovery from Fear. Our fears revolve around certain basic issues—intimacy, risk, failure, loneliness, inadequacy and danger. But God offers us support, empowerment and courage to face fear in all areas of life. This guide will help us discover how God can enable us to face our fears. Six studies, 64 pages, 1160-5.

Recovery from Guilt. Guilt is a distress signal that warns us that something is wrong. If we do not pay attention, we will continue in destructive ways. This guide offers help in working through the pain of what we have done to ourselves and others. Using steps four through nine of the Twelve Steps in conjunction with Scripture, these studies offer hope and help to get beyond guilt to forgiveness. Six studies, 64 pages, 1163-X.

Recovery: A Lifelong Journey. Recovery requires a commitment to keep growing and changing through prayer and discipline. In this guide you'll see how the last three steps of the Twelve Steps provide a model for your lifelong journey of recovery. By following the disciplines of self-awareness, confession, seeking God and asking for guidance, you will find continued healing and growth. Six studies, 64 pages, 1166-4.

Recovery from Loss. Disappointment, unmet expectations, physical or emotional illness and death are all examples of losses that occur in our lives. Working through grief does not help us to forget what we have lost, but it does help us grow in understanding, compassion and courage in the midst of loss. This guide will show you how to receive the comfort God offers. Six studies, 64 pages, 1157-5.

Recovery from Shame. Shame is a social experience. Whatever its source, shame causes people to see themselves as unlovable, unworthy and irreparable. This guide will help you to reform your self-understanding in the light of God's unconditional acceptance. Six studies, 64 pages, 1153-2.

Recovery from Spiritual Abuse. Because of negative teaching we have received, many of us have learned that we have to earn our way with God. We have come to experience the Christian life as a burden—and a source of deep shame. Through these studies, we will discover that we can be healed of spiritual abuse and find freedom and grace in Christ. Six studies, 64 pages, 1159-1.

Recovery from Workaholism. Hard work results in promotions, raises and the respect of colleagues. More important, it fills the need we have to be needed. But overwork also eats away at marriage and family relationships, while making friendships outside the office nearly nonexistent. It can create health problems as well as spiritual struggles. This guide is designed to help you break free of workaholism and accept the rest that God offers. Six studies, 64 pages, 1164-8.